#hustle

a quote book

by gloria marie pelcher

Copyright © 2014 Gloria Marie Pelcher

All rights reserved. No portion of this book may be used or reproduced in any manner whatsoever without written permission of the author or Creative Bluebird except in the case of brief quotations embodied in critical articles and reviews.

The quotes in this book have been collected from multiple sources, and are assumed to be accurate as quoted in their original published forms. Although every effort has been made to verify the quotes and sources, the Publisher cannot guarantee their perfect accuracy. No endorsement of this book has been made by any individual mentioned in this quote book.

#hustle: a quote book

ISBN-13: 978-0692334225 (Creative Bluebird)
ISBN-10: 069233422X

#quotebooks™ is a trademark of

Creative Bluebird
www.creativebluebird.com

For book inquiries please visit
creativebluebird.com/contact

for

___

from

___

date

___

#hustle

Here's to being the hardest working person you know! Success takes hard work, but you are willing to put in the work to make it happen! Hustle. Repeat!

Things may come to those who wait, but only the things left by those who hustle.

Abraham Lincoln

If you work really hard, and you're kind, amazing things will happen.

Conan O'Brien

It's hard to beat a person who never gives up.

> Babe Ruth

Genius is 1% talent and 99% hard work.

Albert Einstein

The three great essentials to achieve anything worthwhile are, first, hard work; second, stick-to-itiveness; third, common sense.

Thomas A. Edison

Happiness is when what you think, what you say, and what you do are in harmony.
    Mahatma Gandhi

Work as hard and as much as you want to on the things you like to do the best.

Richard P. Feynman

I would always rather be happy than dignified.
Charlotte Brontë

Don't wish it were easier. Wish you were better.

Jim Rohn

If you care about what you do and work hard at it, there isn't anything you can't do if you want to.

                                        Jim Henson

There are no shortcuts to any place worth going.
Beverly Sills

Thinking is hard work, which is why you don't see many people doing it.

Sue Grafton

Talent is cheaper than table salt. What separates the talented individual from the successful one is a lot of hard work.

Stephen King

A lot of people want a shortcut. I find the best shortcut is the long way, which is basically two words: work hard.

Randy Pausch

Without hard work, nothing grows but weeds.

        Gordon B. Hinckley

When you chase a dream, you learn about yourself. You learn your capabilities and limitations, and the value of hard work and persistence.

Nicholas Sparks

The difference between ordinary and extraordinary is that little extra.

Jimmy Johnson

No man needs sympathy because he has to work, because he has a burden to carry. Far and away the best prize that life offers is the chance to work hard at work worth doing.

Theodore Roosevelt

Most people work just hard enough not to get fired and get paid just enough money not to quit.

George Carlin

No one ever drowned in sweat.

United States Marine Corps

If you want something you can have it, but only if you want everything that goes with it, including all the hard work and the despair, and only if you're willing to risk failure.

Philip Pullman

...You can do something extraordinary, and something that a lot of people can't do. And if you have the opportunity to work on your gifts, it seems like a crime not to. I mean, it's just weakness to quit because something becomes too hard...
Morgan Matson

Be brave enough to live creatively. The creative is the place where no one else has ever been. You have to leave the city of your comfort and go into the wilderness of your intuition. You cannot get there by bus, only by hard work, risking and by not quite knowing what you are doing. What you will discover will be wonderful: Yourself.

Alan Alda

Don't chase people. Be yourself, do your own thing and work hard. The right people - the ones who really belong in your life - will come to your. And stay.

Will Smith

Everybody has talent, but ability takes hard work.
>
> Michael Jordan

It is easy to hate and it is difficult to love. This is how the whole scheme of things works. All good things are difficult to achieve; and bad things are very easy to get.

Confucius

I'm a greater believer in luck, and I find the harder I work the more I have of it.

Thomas Jefferson

I must learn to be content with being happier than I deserve.

Jane Austen

Hard work beats talent when talent fails to work hard.

Kevin Durant

The backbone of success is...hard work, determination, good planning, and perseverance.

Mia Hamm

Perseverance is the hard work you do after you get tired of doing the hard work you already did.
Newt Gingrich

Happiness is like a butterfly which, when pursued, is always beyond our grasp, but, if you will sit down quietly, may alight upon you.
       Nathaniel Hawthorne

My parents raised me to never feel like I was entitled to success. That you have to work for it. You have to work so hard for it. And sometimes then you don't even get where you need to go.

Taylor Swift

Thinking is the capital, Enterprise is the way, Hard Work is the solution.
A.P.J. Abdul Kalam

Sometimes opportunities float right past your nose. Work hard, apply yourself, and be ready. When an opportunity comes you can grab it.

Julie Andrews Edwards

I'm really very self-confident when it comes to my work. When I take on a project, I believe in it 100%. I really put my soul into it. I'd die for it. That's how I am.

                                                Michael Jackson

Hard work keeps you grounded.

Colleen Houck

Work hard at your job and you can make a living. Work hard on yourself and you can make a fortune.

Jim Rohn

Inspiration is the windfall from hard work and focus. Muses are too unreliable to keep on the payroll.

Helen Hanson

Preparation for tomorrow is hard work today.

Bruce Lee

Belief, hard work, love – you have those things, you can do anything.

Mitch Albom

Hustle isn't just doing the things you love all the time. Hustle is doing the things you don't enjoy sometimes to earn the right to do the things you love.

Jon Acuff

The way to get started is to quit talking and begin doing.
Walt Disney Company

Is there magic in this world? Certainly! But it is not the kind of magic written about in fantasy stories. It is the kind of magic that comes from ideas and the hard work it often takes to make them real.

Robert Fanney

Hard work does not go unnoticed, and someday the rewards will follow.
Allan Rufus

If your dream is a big dream, and if you want your life to work on the high level that you say you do, there's no way around doing the work it takes to get you there.

                                              Joyce Chapman

Be like a duck, paddling and working very hard inside the water, but what everyone sees is a smiling and calm face.

Manoj Arora

Everyone wants to live on top of the mountain, but all the happiness and growth occurs while you're climbing it.

Andy Rooney

Opportunities are usually disguised as hard work, so most people don't recognize them.

Ann Landers

Be honest.
Be kind.
Be honorable.
Work hard.
And always be awesome.
Wil Wheaton

my favorite hustle quote

_____
_____
_____
_____
_____
_____
_____
_____
_____

ABOUT this book

THIS BOOK that you are holding in your hands was made with love by GLORIA MARIE PELCHER. This book is part of the *#quotebooks*™ collection of books. This book is perfectly okay with being loved, bought, read, reread, shared, gifted, tweeted, instagrammed, liked, reviewed, borrowed, and of course quoted.

gloriamarie.com/quotebooks

FB / IG / Twitter: @gloriamarie

www.ingramcontent.com/pod-product-compliance
Lightning Source LLC
Chambersburg PA
CBHW070459050426
42449CB00012B/3046